Historic Bristol

By Anne Crawford, Assistant Archivist, Bristol Record Office.

Bristol's origins and later development differ greatly from those of England's other major historic cities. Unlike them, Bristol had no Roman settlement, it was not an ancient cathedral city nor a county town. It owed its entire existence to trade and manufacture, and this in turn was a direct result of its geographical position.

Originally it was a Saxon settlement in the royal manor of Barton, lying at the junction of the River Avon and its tributary, the Frome, whose meandering course formed an almost complete natural moat and made the site easily defensible. It was protected from seaward attack by the narrow and spectacular gorge of the Avon. From Bristol a network of rivers, the Avon, the Severn, and the Wye, meant that goods could be carried easily into the heart of England, and it lay at the crossroads of three different regions, the south-west, the Midlands and South Wales. This vast hinterland was to prove rich in agricultural, industrial, and mineral products.

On the eve of the Norman Conquest, Bristol was a small but well-established town, whose ships traded extensively with Ireland. Its strategic importance led William the Conqueror to order the building of a castle, which he entrusted to one of his most powerful supporters, Geoffrey, Bishop of Coutances. The lordship of the castle later passed to Robert, Earl of Gloucester, a bastard son of Henry I, and a leading supporter of his half-sister, the Empress Matilda, in her war with King Stephen. Earl Robert was responsible for enlarging the castle into one of the major strongholds of the West. His granddaughter was the first wife of King John and through her the castle passed into royal hands.

The early borough of Bristol was tiny and was divided into four quarters or wards by the four main streets, High Street, Broad Street, Wine Street, and Corn Street. Outside the walls lay the castle, the Benedictine Priory of St James, founded by Earl Robert, the Augustinian abbey founded by Robert

Fitzhardinge, a Bristol burgess of much wealth, and the great Bristol bridge across the Avon, a smaller version of old London Bridge. South of the Avon lay the separate settlement of Redcliffe, with its great church of St Mary (*below*). By the mid twelfth century, a contemporary chronicler could describe Bristol as 'almost the richest city of all in the country, receiving merchandise by ships from lands near and far. It lies in the most fertile part of England and is by its very situation the most strongly fortified of all its cities.'

In the late twelfth and early thirteenth centuries, several factors led to an expansion of the town unparalleled until the eighteenth century. By the mid thirteenth century its port facilities were proving inadequate. The citizens, therefore, embarked on a major programme of harbour improvement based on diverting the River Frome, cutting a new and deeper channel through the marsh near St Augustine's Abbey to join the Avon lower down, and providing on the north side of the channel, opposite St Stephen's church, a new quay for ocean-going ships, which was to become known as Broad Quay (*right*). Other civic improvements included the earliest piped water supply from wells and springs outside the city, and the provision of hospitals for the town's poor and sick, the two most important of which were St Bartholomew's and St Mark's. The earliest almshouses were founded in Long Row by Simon Burton in 1292 and his example was to be followed many times over in succeeding centuries.

Contrairement aux autres grandes villes britanniques. Bristol ne fut fondée ni par les Romains ni autour d'une cathédrale, mais elle doit son existence au commerce saxon et à sa position. Située au point de rencontre de plusieurs rivières (Avon, Frome, Severn, Wye), celles-ci la protégeaient des invasions, tout en assurant les communications avec le reste du pays.

Cette importance stratégique conduisit Guillaume le Conquérant à y faire construire un château, agrandi plus tard par le comte Robert qui en fit l'une des grandes places fortes de l'Ouest, tandis que la cité se développait autour de ses quatre rues principales (High Street, Broad Street, Wine Street, et Corn Street) et que

se construisaient le prieuré bénédictin de St-James, une abbaye et le pont sur l'Avon, version réduite du pont de Londres.

Bristol connut un fort développement à la fin du 12e et au début du 13e siècle. Grâce au détournement de la Frome et à divers aménagements, le port fut considérablement agrandi, tandis que se construisaient les premières canalisations d'eau potable ainsi que des hôpitaux pour les pauvres,

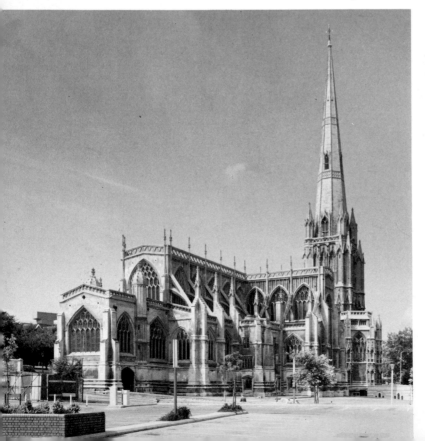

notamment St-Bartholomew's et
St-Marks.

Die Stadt Bristol an der Westküste
Englands ist eine alte, berühmte
Hafenstadt. Wegen dieser gün-
stigen, geographischen Lage sind
Handel und Industrie während
vieler Jahrhunderte immer von
großer Bedeutung gewesen.
   Zuerst siedelten sich die Sachsen
dort an, wo der Fluß Frome in den
Avon fließt. Das Gebiet konnte gut

von allen Seiten verteidigt werden,
denn der verschlungene Frome ist
eine natürliche Vertiefung, und die
schmale, imposante Schlucht des
Avons bietet Schutz gegen Angriff
von der See. Die Flüsse Avon,
Severn und Wye bilden ein aus-
gezeichnetes Netz, um die vielen
Erzeugnisse nach anderen Ländern
und England zu transportieren.
   Wilhelm der Eroberer erkannte
die strategische Bedeutung der
Stadt, und er ließ eine Burg bauen,

Above: **Broad Quay, Bristol,** *by an*
anonymous artist, British School
about 1735. Left: St Mary Redcliffe
from the north-east

Ci-dessus: Broad Quay, Bristol
(Ecole britannique, vers 1735). A
gauche: l'église St-Mary Redcliffe

Oben: Broad Quay, Bristol,
britische Schule ca. 1735. Links:
Die St. Mary Redcliffe Kirche

die später eine wichtige Festung im Westen wurde. Am Anfang war Bristol sehr klein, und die Stadt wurde durch die Hauptstraßen High Street, Broad Street, Wine Street und Corn Street in vier Bezirke geteilt. Außerhalb der Stadtmauern befanden sich die Burg, die benediktinische Priorei St. James und auch die große Bristol Brücke über den Avon. In der Mitte des 12. Jh. gehörte Bristol zu einer der reichsten Städte Englands, weil der Export und Import blühte. Im 13. Jh. wurde der Hafen ausgebaut, weil der alte zu klein war. Ein tieferer Kanal wurde ausgehoben und gegenüber der St. Stephen's Church wurde das Broad Quay angelegt. Andere soziale Einrichtungen betrafen die Wasserversorgung, den Bau von Krankenhäusern und Altersheimen.

The fourteenth century saw the growth of a flourishing cloth industry and Bristol became the major port for the export of woollen cloth. Such was the town's wealth and importance by the end of the century that in 1373 Edward III raised it to a status beyond that of any other provincial city. Bristol was created a county in her own right, with an elective sheriff with his own courts, two burgesses elected to Parliament, and a council of forty to govern with the mayor and sheriff. The boundaries of the new county, carved from Somerset and Gloucestershire, included all the town's existing suburbs and extended down the Avon into the Bristol Channel as far as Flat Holm and Steep Holm. In 1542 Henry VIII created the diocese of Bristol, with the abbey church of St Augustine as the new cathedral, thus making the town truly a city. Although by that date Bristol was little different in size and layout from two centuries earlier, much rebuilding and improvement had taken place. Many of the city churches had been rebuilt, including St Mary Redcliffe, which the munificence of the Canynges family had transformed into 'the fairest, goodliest and most famous parish church in England'. The fine houses of the wealthy merchants and local gentry were scattered throughout the city, cheek by jowl with the homes and shops of poorer men, for there were as yet no fashionable areas where the wealthy congregated. The Dis-

solution of the Monasteries meant that most of their buildings, gardens, and orchards passed into secular use. Much was purchased by the Corporation, including St Mark's Hospital, whose chapel was to become the Lord Mayor's Chapel (right).

During the Civil War in the mid seventeenth century, Bristol's strategic site made it a key to campaigns in the West. In improving the city's defences, the Corporation found the castle, long neglected, was still defensible, but the old city walls could no longer provide adequate protection. It was, therefore, necessary to build a series of earthworks linking the hills surrounding the city, remains of which can still be seen on Brandon Hill. They were broken by a number of forts, the greatest of which, the Royal Fort, was completed by the Royalists under Prince Rupert. The city endured two sieges, in 1643 by the Royalists and in 1645 by the Parliamentary forces, and was considerably damaged. One result of the war was the demolition of the castle in 1656 and the subsequent development of its site.

The city as it appeared at the end of the seventeenth century, at the dawn of its golden age, is well

Right: The Lord Mayor's Chapel, by R. G. and A. W. Reeve, 1832. *Below: the charter granted by Edward III, 8 August 1373*

A droite: La chapelle du Lord Maire *(R. G. et A. W. Reeve, 1832). Ci-dessous: la charte de 1373*

Rechts: Die Kirche des Oberbürgermeisters, von R. G. und A. W. Reeve, 1832. Unten: Der Freibrief von 1373

illustrated by Millerd's map of 1673 (*see inside front cover*). Although by modern standards the city was still tiny, it shows the gradual spread of buildings, outside Lawford's Gate, south of the Avon, and most particularly on the north and western sides, where rich merchants built houses up the slope of St Michael's Hill. There the air was fresh and the view over the city delightful. A little farther to the east the steep incline to the north of Frome Gate had been stepped by the generosity of a citizen named Jonathan Blackwell. Christmas Steps as they are now known and the surrounding buildings are some of the oldest surviving in the city centre. The Marsh, at the farthest end of the spit of land dividing the Avon and the Frome, had been improved earlier in the century, when a bowling-green had been laid out. Among Bristolians it was a favourite place for an evening stroll and on its north-eastern side the development of King Street had begun.

Around the borders of Millerd's map some of the city's most prominent buildings were illustrated. They included the Guildhall, the Castle, the Tolzey courthouse, the Corn Market, and the Merchant Venturers' Hall, none of which now survive. Contemporaries saw Bristol in 1700 as a clean city, particularly in contrast to London, and also as a very fair one.

St Michael's Hill, looking north

St-Michael's Hill, vers le Nord

Der St. Michael's Berg mit Blick nach Norden

Le 14ᵉ siècle vit l'expansion de l'industrie textile et Bristol devint le premier port pour l'exportation des étoffes de laine. Une telle prospérité lui amena l'honneur sans précédent, pour une ville de province, d'être élevée au rang de comté en 1373. Henri VIII dota la ville de son diocèse en 1542, faisant de l'église abbatiale St-Augustine une cathédrale.

Les guerres civiles du 17ᵉ siècle nécessitèrent le renforcement des défenses et une série de fortifications relia les collines entourant la ville; on peut en voir des vestiges sur Brandon Hill. Bristol subit deux sièges (1643 et 1645) qui provoquèrent de nombreux dégâts et la démolition du château.

La carte de Millard de 1673 (*intérieur de la couverture, tête du livre*) montre bien l'état de la ville à l'époque et en particulier l'avancée des constructions au-delà de Lawford's Gate au Sud de l'Avon et vers le Nord et l'Ouest. Un peu plus à l'Est la pente abrupte au Nord de Frome Gate fut dotée d'escaliers par la générosité d'un riche citoyen. Ces escaliers, ainsi que les bâtiments qui les entourent, sont parmi les plus anciennes constructions du centre de Bristol à nous être parvenues. Vers 1700 Bristol

jouissait d'une excellente réputation, étant considérée comme une très belle ville, supérieure à Londres pour sa propreté.

Das Jahr 1373 war bedeutend für die Stadt, den Eduard III. erhob Bristol zu einer Grafschaft, die ihr eigenes Gericht hatte und zwei Bürger zum Parlament in London schicken konnte. Während der Jahrhunderte wuchs der Reichtum Bristols, und Wolle war das wichtigste Exporterzeugnis. Die wohlhabenden Kaufleute bauten schöne Häuser, die man überall in der Stadt finden kann.

Während des Bürgerkrieges im 17. Jh. nahm Bristol eine bedeutende Verteidigungsstellung im Westen ein, und neue Erdwälle mußten gebaut werden, deren Reste man heute noch auf dem Brandon Hill sehen kann.

Zu Beginn des goldenen Zeitalters am Ende des 17. Jh. war Bristol immer noch winzig, aber nach und nach wurden mehr Häuser außerhalb des Lawford's Gate und auch am Hang des St. Michael's Hill gebaut. Jonathan Blackwell ließ die Treppen bauen, die heute als die Christmas Steps bekannt sind, sie werden von Gebäuden umgeben, die heute zu den ältesten in der Stadtmitte gehören. Auf der Karte von Millard aus dem Jahre 1673 kann man das Rathaus, den Tolzey Gerichtshof und den Getreidemarkt sehen, die aber nicht mehr existieren.

The Port of Bristol

The history of the town of Bristol has been synonymous for most of its existence with the growth of the port. It owed its original foundation not just to its defensive position but also to the very safe harbourage provided by the winding Avon Gorge at the cross-roads of the sea and river routes of the Severn Estuary. In the early Middle Ages its trade was mainly with the Viking colonies in Ireland. While most people are familiar with Bristol's role in the African slave trade, few are aware that centuries earlier, its merchants grew rich shipping English slaves to Ireland, a practice which was not stamped out until after the Norman Conquest. The great expansion of the town in the late twelfth century was due primarily to the development of the trade in English wool from sheep raised in the Cotswolds and to the marriage of Henry II and Eleanor of Aquitaine in 1152, which brought to the English Crown her great wine-producing duchy in southern France. By the thirteenth century Gascon wines had almost completely captured the English market and Aquitaine, or Gascony, had become almost completely dependent on England, both for other agricultural products and for manufactured goods. Bristol, as the west's chief port, was ideally situated to take advantage of both factors. Links between Bristol and Bordeaux have remained close to this day, and Harvey's Wine Museum in Denmark Street chronicles the importance of the wine trade to Bristol over the centuries.

In addition to the trade with Ireland and Gascony, Bristol merchants opened up trade with northern France and the Low Countries, then with the Iberian Peninsula and far to the west, with Iceland. The increasing prosperity of the port brought a flourishing shipping and victualling industry as well as the growth of manufacturing industries based on leather imported from Wales and Ireland, iron from the Forest of Dean, lead from the Mendips and, above all, wool from the Cotswolds. It was now English cloth which was exported and not English wool,

Bristol had a large-scale weaving industry and was the major cloth-exporting port; 'Bristol Red' broadcloth was famed as far as the Mediterranean. In contrast to the fourteenth century, the fifteenth was one of depressed trade, chiefly because of the loss of the great Gascon markets when France regained her lost province. Bristol merchants, however, were expanding trade in other directions which were later to bear even greater fruit. Their ships were the first to attempt to break Italian control of the Mediterranean trade, a natural extension to Bristol's increased trade with Spain and Portugal. More important in terms of the future, however, were the first exploratory ventures by Bristol ships westward into the Atlantic. Whether or not Bristol seamen had reached the mainland of North America before John Cabot, who left the port in 1497 on the voyage which discovered Newfoundland, will probably always be a matter for speculation. What is not in doubt is that Bristol's unrivalled position among West Country ports made her the natural entrepôt for American trade.

Trade with the West Indies and North America took most of the sixteenth century to develop and, in the meantime, Bristol's trade continued in its former patterns. Nevertheless some of her leading citizens were among the more active promoters of early colonisation. Sir Ferdinando Gorges, called the 'Father of English Colonisation', used Bristol as his base for many years; John Guy, first Governor of Newfoundland, was a Bristol merchant, and William Penn, the Quaker founder of Pennsylvania, came from a Bristol family. Many of the early emigrants sailed from the port, and after the upheaval of the Civil War more than 10,000 indentured servants from all over the country enrolled their apprenticeships with the city authorities before sailing to Jamaica, Barbados, Virginia, Maryland, Ferdinando Gorges's colony of Maine, or Pennsylvania, where their labour was in great demand. By 1700 Bristol was one of the chief distribution centres for colonial goods, mainly tobacco, sugar, cotton, and rum, and she, in turn, met the colonists' demands for manufactured goods. Great numbers of her citizens ventured any spare cash they had on trade

goods, and the influx of colonial produce led to new industries, chief of which were sugar-refining, and the longer-lived manufacture of tobacco and chocolate.

L'histoire de Bristol est liée à l'expansion de son port, de tous temps d'une grande importance grâce à l'abri naturel des gorges de l'Avon. Avant la conquête normande (1066) son commerce consistait principalement en l'exportation d'esclaves anglais aux colonies Vikings en Irlande. Le 12ᵉ siècle vit le développement du commerce de la laine et celui du vin de Bordeaux après l'annexion de la Gascogne à l'Angleterre, due au mariage d'Henri II et d'Eléonore d'Aquitaine en 1152. Bristol et Bordeaux ont conservé des liens étroits jusqu'à nos jours, comme en témoigne le musée du vin Harvey situé dans Denmark Street.

Au 14ᵉ siècle, le commerce s'étendit au Nord de la France et aux Pays-Bas, puis à la péninsule ibérique et à l'Islande. Les industries de Bristol fructifièrent en conséquence et l'étoffe connue sous le nom de « Bristol Red » était renommée jusqu'en Méditerranée. Le 15ᵉ siècle par contre marqua un arrêt momentané de cette expansion en raison, surtout, du retour de l'Aquitaine à la couronne de France. Avec la découverte de l'Amérique, cependant, de nouvelles tendances se firent jour, la situation de Bristol en faisant le port privilégié du commerce transatlantique et de la colonisation anglaise. Nombreux furent les émigrants qui quittèrent Bristol pour l'Amérique du Nord et, après la guerre civile, c'est de Bristol que partirent les milliers de domestiques pour les Antilles et le Sud des Etats-Unis. Vers 1700 Bristol était un des principaux centres d'importation de denrées coloniales (tabac, sucre, coton et rhum), tandis qu'elle exportait en retour des produits manufacturés.

C'est sur les richesses du commerce avec les Antilles et l'Amérique que « l'age d'or » de Bristol se fonda, et notamment la tristement célèbre traite des esclaves au 18ᵉ siècle, effectuée sur la base d'un voyage triangulaire. Des produits manufacturés partaient pour l'Afrique occidentale qui les échangeait pour des esclaves. Ces derniers étaient alors transportés en Amérique et aux Antilles où ils étaient échangés pour les produits de ces régions, ceux-ci étant ensuite ramenés en Angleterre. L'aspect inhumain de ce commerce fut de plus en plus critiqué vers la fin du 18e siècle et Bristol devint un centre actif du mouvement pour la l'abolition de l'esclavage.

C'est alors que le port de Bristol connut son déclin. Les guerres d'indépendance des Etats-Unis et l'expansion de la marine américaine y contribuèrent. Le commerce du tabac passa à Glasgow tandis que les équipements supérieurs du port de Liverpool attiraient de plus en plus de navires, malgré les efforts de Bristol pour se moderniser. Ce n'est qu'avec la construction d'installations portuaires à Avonmouth et Portishead, des deux côtés de l'embouchure de l'Avon, à la fin du 19e siècle, que le port de Bristol recommença à recouvrer sa prospérité.

Der Hafen gehört zu den bedeutendsten Merkmalen der Stadt. Er wurde nicht nur wegen der guten Verteidigungsposition gebaut sondern auch weil die Schlucht des Avons so ungefährlich ist. Im frühen Mittelalter wurde hauptsächlich mit Irland gehandelt. Am Ende des 12. Jh. trat die große Expansion der Stadt ein, die an dem Wollhandel und der Heirat zwischen Heinrich II. und Eleanor von Aquitanien lag. Fast der ganze Wein, aber auch andere landwirtschaftliche Erzeugnisse der Gascogne wurden nach Bristol exportiert. In Harvey's Weinmuseum in Denmark Street kann man die Bedeutung des Weinhandels während der Jahrhunderte sehen.

Die Kaufleute Bristols handelten auch mit Nordfrankreich, den Niederlanden und Spanien. Trotz der verschiedenen Erzeugnisse war Wolle am wichtigsten, und Bristol wurde der bedeutendste Wollstoffexporthafen. Im 15. Jh. ging der Handel zurück, denn Frankreich hatte die Gascogne zurückerobert, aber die Kaufleute eröffneten den Handel mit Nordamerika, der später noch größeren Reichtum brachte. Viele Bürger aus Bristol kolonisierten die westindischen In-

Right: **Departure of Cabot,** *watercolour by E. Board, 1906*

A droite: le départ de Cabot *(E. Board, 1906)*

Rechts: Die Abreise des Seefahrers Cabot, *von E. Board, 1906*

seln und Teile Nordamerikas. Bristol wurde der Importhafen für Tabak, Zucker, Baumwolle und Rum und der Exporthafen für Fertigwaren, die zu den Kolonien geschickt wurden.

Dieser Handel brachte im 18. Jh. großen Reichtum mit sich, und dazu gehörte auch der Sklavenhandel. Die Schiffe fuhren nach Afrika mit Gewehren, wertlosem Schmuck und Rum als Austausch gegen Sklaven, die dann über den Atlantik verschifft wurden, und die Schiffe kamen mit Erzeugnissen aus den Kolonien zurück. Am Ende des Jahrhunderts merkten die Kaufleute Bristols, daß dieser Handel unmenschlich war, und die Sklavenschiffe legten von dann ab in Liverpool an.

Nach dem amerikanischen Unabhängigkeitskrieg ging der Handel stark zurück. Amerikanische Schiffe transportierten mehr

Güter, außerdem konnten Schiffe über 150 t nicht den Avon hinauffahren. Versuche wurden unternommen, die Anlagen auszubauen, und der Hafen wurde zwischen 1804 und 1809 modernisiert. Aber erst nachdem die Docks in Avonmouth 1877 und die in Portishead 1879 gebaut worden waren, konnte Bristol den Handel zurückgewinnen.

It was on the prosperity generated by trade with the West Indies and America that Bristol's golden age was based. One branch of this trade which achieved great notoriety was the slave trade. It was based on a triangular voyage carrying trade goods such as trinkets, blankets, guns, and rum to West Africa, where they were exchanged for slaves. The slaves were then shipped across the Atlantic and on the last leg of the voyage colonial

goods were brought back to Bristol. During most of the eighteenth century, the slave trade was regarded as providing an essential supply of labour to the colonies. Contrary to popular opinion, very few slaves came to Bristol and most of those that did so came as body servants to plantation-owners. In the last decades of the century the conscience of Bristol merchants was slowly roused against the inhumanity of the trade and the Anti-Slavery movement became very active in the city, while domination of the trade passed to Liverpool.

The end of the eighteenth century saw the port of Bristol in decline. The American War of Independence cut off its most lucrative trade and after the war, more goods were carried in American ships, the tobacco trade passed to Glasgow, and the far superior

Left: The Floating Harbour, Bristol, *watercolour by C. P. Knight, 1879. Below: the S.S.* Great Britain *illuminated at night. Previous page:* View of Clifton Hill from the Sea Banks, *watercolour by N. Pocock, 1781*

A gauche: le port flottant, Bristol *(C. P. Knight, 1879). Ci-dessous: le S.S.* Great Britain. *Page précédente:* Vue de Clifton Hill des Sea Banks *(N. Pocock, 1781)*

Links: Pontons im Hafen, Bristol *von C. P. Knight, 1879. Unten: Der Dampfer 'Great Britain'. Vorhergehende Seite:* Blick auf den Clifton Berg vom Seeufer, *von N. Pocock, 1781*

It was not until 1970 that the *Great Britain*, then a rotting hulk, was brought back to Bristol from the Falkland Islands to be restored to her former glory. The battle to establish docks at Avonmouth was long and involved, but it was not until they were built in 1877, with another set on the opposite bank of the river mouth at Portishead in 1879, that Bristol's prosperity as a port began to recover, but it never regained its former pre-eminence. Unlike Liverpool, it did not become a major passenger port, though many of its ships carried passengers as well as cargo. Shipbuilding continued in the city well into the twentieth century, but the ships produced were all small by modern standards, those for the Royal Navy, for instance, were rarely larger than gunboats. The docks at Avonmouth were expanded with the opening of the Royal Edward Dock in 1908 and the Royal Portbury Dock in 1977. The City Docks were effectively closed to commercial traffic by the late 1970s, leaving the city's waterways to be developed for leisure-time activities.

S.S. GREAT BRITAIN

port facilities of Liverpool attracted shipping away from Bristol. The winding Avon, which had once meant superb security for the growing port now made it unsuitable for ships of more than 150 tons to come up the river beyond Hungroad. Various attempts to improve facilities like new quays and a dry dock failed to solve the problem, and it was not until the construction of the Floating Harbour and the New Cut, built between 1804 and 1809, that the port was effectively modernised. The benefits of modernisation were unfortunately nullified by the prohibitively high harbour dues charged to recoup the cost. It was a severe blow to civic pride when Bristol's two great steamships, the *Great Western* and the *Great Britain*, once built, were never able to return to their home port, but operated out of Liverpool instead.

The Georgian Age and Beyond

The eighteenth century has rightly been described as Bristol's golden age. The wealth generated by her dominance of the American trade permeated down to all save her poorest class of citizens, as witness the abundance of Georgian housing of all types which survives in the city. In 1700 it still had a medieval appearance, with its jumble of timber-framed buildings and only small areas of new development outside the old city bounds. By 1830, its population had more than trebled, swollen by immigrants from all over the British Isles and beyond. The old city had been largely rebuilt and had expanded to twice its size, with extensive new suburbs at Clifton, Bedminster, and in the east, as well as up the slopes of Kingsdown to the north. The introduction of squares, begun in 1699 with Queen Square, was an imitation of London planning, but being both healthy and visually attractive soon became very popular. Queen Square was the first, the largest, and for most of the century the most important, for many of the wealthiest merchants had houses there, the Corporation chose one house to be the Mayor's mansion house and also built a fine Customs House. Both these buildings were burned in the great Reform Bill riots of 1831. The development of Hotwells as a fashionable spa began early in the century, and was followed by the growth of Clifton as a spa in its own right.

Clifton never seriously rivalled Bath as a resort for the fashionable world, but it did bring quite a different class of society to Bristol, hitherto almost completely mercantile and serious-minded in its outlook. The Theatre Royal was built in 1766, and a new Music Room in nearby Prince Street, assembly rooms and pump rooms all diverted citizens and visitors alike. While never renowned for its

Le 18e siècle a été fort justement appelé « l'âge d'or » de Bristol. La ville, enrichie par le commerce avec les Etats-Unis se couvrit de nouvelles constructions de style anglais classique (georgien). Entre 1700 et 1830 Bristol tripla sa population et doubla de superficie. Les « squares » en vogue à l'époque s'y construisirent sur le modèle de ceux de Londres, Queen Square étant le premier et pendant longtemps le plus important. C'est également à cette époque que Hotwells et Clifton, deux banlieues de Bristol, acquirent leur réputation en tant que villes d'eau. Bien qu'elle n'ait jamais pu prétendre rivaliser d'élegance avec Bath, Clifton attira à Bristol une société plus mondaine et artistique. Le Theatre Royal (1766), la Music Room dans Prince Street, ainsi que les Assembly Rooms et Pump Rooms furent érigées pour distraire cette nouvelle clientèle. Le poète Coleridge résida à Bristol qui abrita aussi une école de peintres paysagistes.

Das 18. Jh. ist mit Recht als das goldene Zeitalter Bristols beschrieben worden. Die meisten Bürger wurden wegen des nord- amerikanischen Handels reich, und die georgianischen Häuser bezeugen das. Die alte Stadt mußte völlig umgebaut werden, und die neuen Vororte wie Clifton, Bedminster und viele andere mehr entstanden. Der Queen Square war der erste Platz, der in Bristol angelegt wurde, und viele reiche Kaufleute bauten Häuser hier. Später wurde Clifton ein Heilbad, das viel und gerne besucht wurde.

Das Theatre Royal wurde im Jahre 1766 gebaut und auch ein neuer Musiksaal in der Prince Street, dies zog viele Künstler an. Es gab auch eine Landschaftsmalerakademie, und Francis Danby und Edward Bird waren die bekanntesten Maler.

Left: Queen Square, *watercolour by T. L. S. Rowbotham, 1827*
Below: the Theatre Royal

A gauche: Queen Square *(T. L. S. Rowbotham, 1827)*
Ci-dessous: le Theatre Royal

Links: Queen Square von T. L. S. Rowbotham, 1827
Unten: Das Theatre Royal

contribution to English culture, Bristol, nevertheless, gave shelter to Coleridge and Southey, gave birth to Thomas Chatterton and Hannah More, and produced its own school of landscape artists, headed by Francis Danby and Edward Bird.

Yet the heart of Bristol was still its commerce, just as at the physical heart of the city lay the Quay on the Frome, a street for ships, which existed until nearly the end of the nineteenth century, when the Frome was covered to form the modern Centre. The view of ships' masts and church towers which met the eye from any of the surrounding hills never failed to delight visitors and was a frequent source of inspiration for local artists.

The eighteenth century saw, too, a great expansion in Bristol's industry. The ready source of coal at Kingswood and elsewhere in the immediate vicinity of the city encouraged the building of lead and gunshot works, iron-founding, and at Baptist Mills the first brass foundry in the country. Shipbuilding, both for the Royal Navy and the mercantile marine, continued to flourish. Industries associated with colonial produce such as sugar, tobacco, and cocoa have already been mentioned, but it is worth noting that the Wills tobacco firm and Fry's chocolate factories, which continued to be among Bristol's largest employers until well into the twentieth century, were both companies founded in the eighteenth century.

Distilleries, clay-pipe manufactories, soap-making, salt-refining, cotton manufacture, all these flourished. So, too, did glass-making. The city's window glass was considered to be the best in the country, bottles for distilleries, for wine, for spa water, were made in large quantities, but Bristol was perhaps most famed for its 'blue glass'. Pottery manufacture produced another blue, Bristol's imitation Delft ware. As a distribution centre for its own manufactures as well as colonial goods and European imports, Bristol dominated the south-west, South Wales, and the southern Midlands. With its widespread network of rivers, it was but little affected by the Canal Age, but the coming of the railways was another matter. Isambard

Kingdom Brunel has always occupied a special niche in the hearts of Bristolians. The grace of the Clifton Suspension Bridge (1864), the engineering marvels of the two pioneering steamships, the *Great Western* (1838) and the *Great Britain* (1843), and the Great Western Railway, linking Bristol and London (1841), all justify this, and the city has recently seen the opening of the Brunel Engineering Centre Trust, set up to restore Brunel's terminus for his Great Western Railway at Temple Meads.

Bristol au 18ᵉ siècle connut aussi un développement industriel, notamment les industries métallurgiques, les constructions navales, le traitement des produits exo-

Left: Old Floating Dock, Hotwell Road *by T. L. S. Rowbotham, c. 1827. Below: Bristol blue glass. Previous page:* View of the Avon Gorge, *watercolour by F. Danby, c. 1823*

A gauche: Vieux dock flottant, Hotwell Road *(T. L. S. Rowbotham, vers 1827). Ci-dessous: le verre bleu de Bristol. Page précédente:* Vue sur la gorge de l'Avon *(F. Danby, 1823)*

Links: Das alte schwimmende Dock, Hotwell Road, *von T. L. S. Rowbotham ca. 1827. Unten: Bristols blaues Glas. Vorhergehende Seite:* Blick auf die Schlucht des Avon, *von F. Danby, 1823*

zweigen. Glasherstellung ist auch erwähnenswert, und Bristol ist wahrscheinlich am besten wegen des „blauen Glases" bekannt. Bristol dominierte als Hauptverteilungszentrum im Südwesten, in Südwales und Südmittelengland. Ein sehr bedeutender Mann, der die Herzen aller Leute in Bristol gewann, war Isambard Kingdom Brunel, der die Clifton Hängebrücke 1864, die bahnbrechenden

Dampfschiffe „Great Western" und „Great Britain" 1838 bzw. 1843 sowie die „Great Western Railway", die Eisenbahnverbindung zwischen Bristol und London, gebaut hat. Vor kurzem ist ein Brunel Trust ins Leben gerufen worden, um seinen Bahnhof in Temple Meads zu restaurieren. Die „Great Britain" ist auch restauriert worden, und sie kann besichtigt werden.

Throughout the Georgian period, the spiritual life of the city was dominated by the Nonconformists. The Society of Friends had existed since the seventeenth century, and a disproportionately high number of the most influential city families, like the Frys, Harfords, Champions, and Lloyds, came from the small group of Quakers. The Baptists, too, had flourished from the seventeenth century, while by the end of the eighteenth century the Unitarians, with their chapel at Lewins Mead were particularly prominent. The first legal wedding in a Nonconformist chapel took place in the Congregational Brunswick Square Chapel in 1837. Prior to that marriages could only be

tiques (sucre, tabac et cacao), les savonneries, les textiles et la verrerie, Bristol étant renommée pour son « verre bleu ». La ville était alors la capitale de Sud-Ouest de l'Angleterre, du Sud du Pays de Galles et du Sud des Midlands. L'arrivée des chemins de fer (1841) la transforma aussi et le grand ingénieur Brunel dota Bristol de nombreux ouvrages dont le célèbre pont suspendu de Clifton.

Im 18. Jh. wurden unter anderem Bleifabriken, Eisenhütten und die erste Messinggießerei eröffnet, und die königliche und Handelsmarine ließ Schiffe bauen. Die berühmten Wills Tabakfirma und Fry's Schokoladenfabriken, die im 18. Jh. gegründet wurden, gehören zu den bedeutendsten Industrie-

Above: Clifton Suspension Bridge, watercolour by S. Jackson, 1831.

Brunel's design for the famous Clifton Suspension Bridge was chosen in 1831. It had a strong Egyptian air and the columns were crowned with sphinxes. Brunel commissioned Samuel Jackson to show potential subscribers to the project how his bridge would appear in its natural surroundings. Most of the painting is by Jackson but the architectural features are by a different hand, presumably that of Brunel himself. Building work started in 1836 but soon ran into financial difficulties. It was not completed until 1864, to a somewhat altered design. That it was finished at all was Bristol's tribute to the memory of Brunel.

Ci-dessus: Le pont suspendu de Clifton *(aquarelle de S. Jackson, 1831).*

Les plans de l'ingénieur Brunel furent acceptés la même année, ce tableau étant destiné à attirer les souscripteurs. Les travaux commencèrent en 1836 mais le pont ne fut terminé qu'en 1864 avec quelques changements aux plans originaux.

Oben: Die Clifton Hängebrücke, Aquarell von S. Jackson, 1831.

Brunels Entwurf für die Brücke wurde 1831 gewählt. Er gab Jackson den Auftrag, um potentiellen Befürwortern des Projektes zu zeigen, wie diese Brücke in der natürlichen Umgebung aussehen würde. Die Bauarbeiten dauerten von 1836 bis 1864, und der Entwurf wurde geändert.

performed in Anglican churches. John Wesley and George Whitefield began their Methodist preaching to the godless miners of Kingswood, and Wesley's New Room in Broadmead was the first Methodist chapel to be built in the country. The rapidly increasing population led to the formation of two new Anglican parishes, those of St George in the east of the city in 1751 and St Paul's, Portland Square, for the fashionable new residential area north of St James, in 1787. From the mid nineteenth century the combination of a religious revival and a population explosion led to scores of new churches and chapels as well as two cathedrals, both for the new Roman Catholic diocese of Clifton; the second, only a few years old, stands in Pembroke Road.

Long before the Georgian period Bristol had been noted for the extent of its charities. The medieval foundations of hospitals and almshouses were early evidence of this, but after the Reformation, philanthropists large and small poured out their money, particularly on the foundation of schools and the care of the poor and sick. The Grammar School was founded in 1532, the Cathedral School in 1542, Queen Elizabeth's Hospital a few years later, and Red

Maids, revolutionary in that it was for girls, in 1634. All are now flourishing independent schools. By 1700 there were six new sets of almshouses, a public library in King Street, and a central workhouse and hospital, later known as St Peter's Hospital, had been established for those on parish relief. The Royal Infirmary, established in 1737 by public subscription, was one of the first of its

kind outside London. Bristol's most munificent benefactor in the eighteenth century was Edward Colston. He founded almshouses on St Michael's Hill, a new school for one hundred boys which was named after him, a charity school in Temple, the parish of his birth, and was responsible for many lesser benefactions. In later centuries only the Wills family have approached Colston's generosity.

Sur le plan religieux, Bristol au 18e siècle a surtout été un centre des religions dites « non conformistes », telles que les quakers et les méthodistes, dont la première chapelle (Wesley's New Room) fut construite à Broadmead. Le milieu du 19e siècle connut une renaissance religieuse et de nombreuses églises de toutes dénominations furent construites, dont deux cathédrales catholiques.

De tous temps Bristol a abrité de généreux philantropes qui ont doté la ville d'hôpitaux, hospices et écoles, dont les plus notables sont la Grammar School (1532), la Cathedral School (1542) et Red Maids, école de filles (1634) et le Royal Infirmary (1737), un des premiers hôpitaux de ce type hors de Londres. Le plus généreux bienfaiteur de Bristol au 18e siècle, Edward Colston, légua à la ville un hospice, une nouvelle école de garçons qui porte son nom, et bien d'autres œuvres de charité.

Während der georgianischen Zeit wurde das geistliche Leben von Dissidenten dominiert. Die Gesellschaft der Freunde existierte bereits im 17. Jh., und ein unmäßig großer Teil der einflußreichen Familien Bristols gehörte der Quäkergruppe an. Es gab auch Baptisten und Unitarier und John Wesley, Gründer der Methodistenkirche, began seinen Kreuzzug durch ganz England. Von der Mitte des 19. Jh. an wurden viele neue Kirchen und Kapellen sowie zwei katholische Kathedralen in Clifton und in Pembroke Road gebaut.

Bristol hatte schon vor vielen Jahrhunderten wohltätige Einrichtungen gebaut, dazu gehörten viele Schulen, Altersheime, Krankenhäuser und eine Bibliothek.

Above left: Temple Meads Station, about 1845. Left: Lewin's Mead Chapel, entrance front. Above right: St Peter's Hospital c. 1850. Right: Colston's Almshouses

Ci-dessus à gauche: la gare de Temple Meads, vers 1845. A gauche: la chapelle Lewin's Mead. Ci-dessus à droite: l'hôpital St-Peter's, vers 1850. A droite: l'hospice de Colston

Oben links: Der Bahnhof Temple Meads, ca. 1845. Links: Die Mead Kirche von Lewin. Oben rechts: St. Peter's Hospital, ca. 1850. Rechts: Die Altersheime von Colston

Bristol's Buildings

Until 1939 the whole variety of English urban architecture could be surveyed in Bristol with its medieval street pattern, large numbers of timber-framed buildings, Georgian squares and terraces, Victorian commercial and industrial buildings and suburban villas. The devastation of the Blitz destroyed the eastern half of the old city and much of what survived the bombs was swept away by post-war planners, but a wealth of interesting buildings still remain, many of them already referred to here.

There is little medieval work in Bristol now that is not ecclesiastical. The Cathedral and St Mary Redcliffe are the outstanding examples, but the chapel of St Mark's Hospital, now the Lord Mayor's Chapel, the priory church of St James, and St Stephen, with its beautiful tower, are all worth seeing. The tower of St John the Baptist rises above the only surviving medieval gateway into the town and St Nicholas, by Bristol Bridge, now houses the ecclesiastical section of the City Museum. Very little Tudor or Stuart domestic building can be seen now, but the bottom of Christmas Steps, with the gateway of St Bartholomew's Hospital, gives a tantalising glimpse of what the old heart of the city was once like. Sir John Young's Great House, where he entertained Queen Elizabeth I, has gone (Colston Hall now stands upon the site), but its lodge higher up the hill, the Red Lodge, with its magnificent panelled interiors, is now part of the City Museum. The 'Llandoger Trow' in King Street and some of the earlier houses on St Michael's Hill, with a few other isolated examples, are sole representatives of countless sixteenth- and seventeenth-century buildings which survived until the mid twentieth century. The finest was St Peter's Hospital, reconstructed in 1612 for Mayor Robert Aldworth, and destroyed in the Blitz. From the end of the seventeenth century date two of the most attractive sets of almshouses, those of the Merchant Venturers in King Street and of Edward Colston on St Michael's Hill.

With the new Georgian squares and terraces came a new building material, brick. King Street, Prince Street, and Queen Square all contain fine examples of early eighteenth-century houses, particularly Nos. 66–70 Prince Street, 6 King Street, and 29 and 37 Queen Square. Dowry Square, Hotwells,

Left: St John-on-the-wall, steeple and St John's Gate. Below: the 'Llandoger Trow'

A gauche: l'église St-John-on-the-wall. Ci-dessous: le pub 'Llandoger Trow'

Links: Die Kirche St. John-on-the-wall. Unten: Das Wirtshaus 'Llandoger Trow'

is another beautiful early Georgian square, while Orchard Street, just off College Green, is the most complete surviving street of the period. In the business heart of the city, John Wood designed the Exchange in Corn Street in 1743 as a place for merchants to meet. Outside it are the four great bronze 'nails', or trading tables, that are believed to be the origin of the expression 'to pay on the nail'. Farther down Corn Street are the Commercial Rooms, modelled on Lloyd's Coffee House in London. The Old Council House, designed by Robert Smirke and completed in 1827, stands on the corner of High Street and Broad Street, replacing an earlier council house on the same site built in 1704. It was in its turn replaced as the seat of civic government by the new Council House on College Green, in 1956.

Bristol pouvait se vanter de posséder, jusqu'en 1939, un échantillonage complet de l'histoire architecturale anglaise. Les bombardements de la 2e guerre mondiale malheureusement détruisirent la moitié Est de la ville et les modernisations de l'après-guerre firent disparaître de nombreux autres bâtiments anciens. On peut cependant encore en admirer un grand nombre.
Parmi les monuments religieux du moyen-âge on remarquera la cathédrale anglicane, l'église St-Mary Redcliffe, la Lord Mayor's Chapel et les églises St-James et St-Stephen, ainsi que St-John the Baptist et St-Nicholas. De l'architecture domestique de l'époque Tudor il reste peu; on peut encore admirer l'entrée de l'hôpital St-Bartholomew au bas des Christmas

Above right: The Exchange, main front. Right: Redland Chapel. Opposite page: Park Street and the University Tower. Overleaf: Royal York Crescent

Ci-dessus á droite: l'ancienne bourse du commerce. A droite: la chapelle Redland. Page opposée: Park Street et la Tour Université. Page suivante: Royal York Crescent

Oben rechts: Die Getreidebörse. Rechts: die Redland Kirche. Gegenüberliegende Seite: Park Street und der Universität Turm. Umseitig: Royal York Crescent

Steps et Red Lodge qui contient de magnifiques boiseries. Du 16ᵉ siècle ont survécu The Llandoger Trow dans King Street et quelques maisons sur St-Michael's Hill. De la fin du 17ᵉ siècle datent le charmant hospice des Merchant Venturers dans King Street et celui d'Edward Colston sur St-Michael's Hill.

L'ère georgienne amena les constructions en brique, dont on peut admirer des exemples en particulier dans King Street, Prince Street et Queen Square; voir aussi Dowry Square à Hotwells et Orchard Street, l'Exchange (1743), les Commercial Rooms et, au coin de High Street et Broad Street, Old Council House (1827).

Vor dem letzten Kriege konnte man in Bristol Häuser, Geschäfte und Plätze im Stil der verschiedenen Jahrhunderte sehen, von denen viele im Kriege zerstört oder von modernen Planern abgerissen worden sind, trotzdem gibt es noch eine Fülle an interessanten Gebäuden.

Die Kathedrale und die Kirche St. Mary Redcliffe sind einmalige Beispiele aus dem Mittelalter. Die Kapelle des St. Mark's Hospitals, die Kirchen St. James und St. Stephen mit dem schönen Turm sind alle sehenswert. Der Torweg von St. Bartholomew's Hospital unten bei den Christmas Steps erinnert daran, wie die alte Stadtmitte ausgesehen hat. Red Lodge, Teil des City Museums, ist wegen der prächtigen Holzwände bemerkenswert. Die attraktiven Altersheime der Merchant Venturers in King Street und von Edward Colston auf dem St. Michael's Hill stammen aus dem 17. Jh.

Die Häuser Nr. 66–70 in Prince Street, Nr. 6 in King Street und Nr. 29 sowie 37 in Queen Street gehören zu den besten Beispielen des frühen 18. Jh. Dowry Square, Hotwells, ist auch ein schöner Platz

aus der Zeit der Könige Georg, und Orchard Street ist die kompletteste Straße dieses Zeitalters. Im Geschäftszentrum steht die Börse aus dem Jahre 1743 und sehenswert sind die vier großen Bronzenägel.

During the course of the eighteenth century, several small country seats were built by successful Bristol merchants in neighbouring villages which have since become absorbed into the city. These include Redland Court with its exquisite chapel (now a parish church), Goldney House, Clifton Hill House, Royal Fort House, and Blaise Castle House. King's Weston House, designed by Vanbrugh, and Ashton Court, originally a sixteenth-century house with many later additions, were both gentlemen's

homes close to the city. Country homes, however, were owned by very few of Bristol's merchant fraternity. Far more typical is the house of John Pinney, built for him in Great George Street, and now known as the Georgian House. It is run by the City Museum as a museum of eighteenth-century town life. The terraces of Clifton, rising tier above tier from the river are later in date, though many individual Clifton houses date from the mid eighteenth century. Bristol's natural conservatism, in architecture as in much else, ensured that the Georgian styles lingered well into the nineteenth century, and there are numerous pleasing streets of terraces and villas in the prosperous northern and western suburbs of the city.

Bristol's public buildings of the nineteenth century cannot compare with those of the great northern industrial cities. There is nothing on a grand scale. The Victoria Rooms, the Royal West of England Academy of Art, the original city museum, modelled on the Doge's Palace in Venice and now used as the University Refectory, the new City Museum and Art Gallery next door, all in Queen's Road, lead the eye on to a truly dominating building, the University Tower. Designed in the 1920s by Sir George Oatley in the Gothic style, its position at the top of the steeply rising Park Street is one that cannot fail to impress. Only a few hundred yards away, on Brandon Hill, close to the remains of Civil War fortifications, is another tower. The Cabot Tower was erected in 1897 to commemorate the four hundredth anniversary of

Left: the Cabot Tower
Above: the statue of Neptune
Right: the Welsh Back, Bristol's City Docks

A gauche: la tour Cabot
Ci-dessus: la statue de Neptune
A droite: bateau-phare dans les docks

Links: Der Cabot Turm
Oben: Die Neptune Statue
Rechts: Feuerschiff in den Docks

Bristol's City Docks at night

Les docks de Bristol la nuit

Bristols Docks bei Nacht

John Cabot's discovery of New-foundland. Like many other ports, Bristol has a legacy of redundant waterside warehouses. In recent years many of them have taken on a new lease of life and now house an Industrial Museum, a modern art centre, a Lifeboat Museum, and an exhibition complex as well as cafés and shops. The finest of them all, built as a granary in the Bristol Venetian manner, is a jazz club. All are part of a highly successful attempt to put new life and vigour into the area of the old city docks in a way that satisfies both residents and visitors alike.

Les riches marchands de Bristol se firent construire quelques grandes demeures; notamment Redland Court avec son exquise chapelle, Goldney House, Clifton Hill House, Royal Fort House, Blaise Castle House, King's Weston House, Ashton Court et la Georgian House dans Great George Street, maintenant un musée de la vie au 18e siècle. Les « terraces » de Clifton sont également à voir, ainsi

que de nombreuses rues dans les quartiers Nord et Ouest de la ville.

L'architecture victorienne est relativement moins bien représen-tée; on peut voir cependant les Victoria Rooms, la Royal West of England Academy of Art, le Uni-versity Refectory, le City Museum et Art Gallery, tous dans Queen's Road et la University Tower, construite dans les années 1920 dans le style « gothique » victorien. La Cabot Tower fut érigée en 1897. Comme tous les ports, Bristol compte de nombreux entrepôts vides. Un grand effort de rénova-tion et de conversion a été fait récemment pour renouveler le quartier des anciens docks où l'on trouve notamment un musée de l'industrie, un centre d'art moderne, des cafés, des boutiques et un club de jazz.

Im 18. Jh. wurden mehrere Land-häuser von den reichen Kaufleuten in Bristol gebaut, und dazu ge-hören Redland Court mit der sehr feinen Kapelle, Goldney House, Clifton Hill House, Royal Fort House und Blaise Castle House. Im Georgian House in Great George Street befindet sich das Museum, wo das Stadtleben im 18. Jh. zeigt wird. Viele Häuser in Clifton stam-men aus der Mitte des 18. Jh., aber

die Häuserreihen am Fluß wurden später gebaut. Es lohnt sich durch die vielen Straßen in den nörd-lichen und westlichen Vororten zu gehen, weil man hier viele interess-ante Häuser findet.

Die Victoria Rooms, die Royal West of English Academy of Art, das alte Stadtmuseum, ein Modell des Dogen Palastes in Venedig und heute die Mensa der Universität, und das neue City Museum und die Kunstgallerie nebenan in Queen's Road führen zu dem wirklich dominierenden University Tower von 1920, ein Turm, der im goti-schen Stil gebaut worden ist. Er steht oben auf der steilen Park Street. Der Cabot Tower wurde 1897 zur Erinnerung an John Cabot errichtet, der 4 Jahrhun-derte früher Neufundland entdeckt hatte. In Bristol findet man viele leerstehende Lagerhäuser am Flußufer, in denen jetzt Re-staurants, Läden, ein Industriemu-seum und andere Ausstellungs-komplexe untergebracht sind. In dem schönsten von allen, das im venezianischen Bristolstil gebaut worden ist, findet man heute einen Jazzklub. Man hat erfolgreich die Docks ausgebaut, um diesem Stadtteil wieder Leben und Vitali-tät zu verleihen.